Vintage Designs

Cut & Collage

Vintage Designs

SIRIUS

This edition published in 2025 by Sirius Publishing, a division of
Arcturus Publishing Limited,
26/27 Bickels Yard, 151–153 Bermondsey Street,
London SE1 3HA

ISBN: 978-1-3988-5787-2
AD012981NT

Printed in China

INTRODUCTION

The power to travel through time and create your own vintage art is right at your fingertips—just cut out the images and watch your timeless world come to life. Complete with unique people, historic places, and antique objects, this cut and collage book contains hundreds of images to inspire you.

Collaging is a wonderful and relaxing way to build your own special world, add some wonder to a journal, or even make your diary more exciting. Once you have your base material in hand, all you need to do is flip through these pages and start creating. You can use the images as small details in any of your existing projects or craft an entirely new piece. There are no limits or rules here—just you and your imagination.

Materials needed for collage:

Base material

A sheet of paper, a canvas, journal, or any other flat material will do. The thicker the paper, the easier it will be to layer your images.

Glue or tape

A glue stick, clear-dry liquid craft glue, or double-sided tape will keep your images in place.

Scissors

Any pair of scissors will suffice to cut out the images, but a hobby knife might be needed for more precision.

Additional materials for decoupage:

Decorative object

Use something like a pot plant, dish, or other decorative object as the base for your project.

Top coat

A varnish or lacquer is needed to ensure smoothness and preserve the integrity of your piece.

Paintbrush

A brush is needed to apply your top coat evenly. Additionally, it might be useful to use a brush and a liquid glue to secure your images for decoupage.

How to Collage

1.
With your base material ready to go, it's time to start collaging. Flip through the book until you find an image that speaks to you—it's best to start with a bigger one to build on. Using your scissors or hobby knife, carefully cut out the image and position it on the base. Reposition it as needed until you're happy with how it looks, then glue or tape it down.

2.
Once you have your first piece secured, it's time to start building around it. You can cut out your images all at once or one at a time, depending on your vision. Try to vary the size and look of your images as you go along. Part of the fun is making it as unique as possible.

3.
With your next piece(s) ready, start expanding your image. Layers are crucial in collaging as they add interest and depth to the project, so don't be afraid to get creative with it. Make dynamic scenes in front of historic landmarks or create your own vintage postcard—let the images guide you.

4.
If you're new to the art, try arranging all of the collected images without adhesive until you're happy with their placement—if they're glued down, it's hard to make any tweaks or changes. If you have other items handy, such as newspaper clippings or magazine images, you can add these to your piece as well for a varied, textured look.

5.
Once your collage feels complete, secure all the images with your adhesive and proudly display your art.

6.
These images can be used for a myriad of projects, not just collage.

7.
If you're working on a decoupage piece, repeat the process on a decorative object—a vase, a dish, or a piece of furniture—instead of a flat base material. Once you've set your images, go over your work with a lacquer or varnish to ensure that everything is evenly textured and properly sealed.

8.
For scrapbooking, use the images as details around your pictures to add a touch of whimsy to your memories.

Collage big or small—as long as you're having fun and letting your imagination be your guide.

Government
Power Delegated
For the
Happiness
Of
Mankind
Conducted
by
Wisdom
Justice
And
Mercy
American Congress

U.S. NAVY
JOHN STEPHENSON
NEW YORK
UNITED STATES

AYER'S CHERRY PECTORAL
There's nothing so bad for a Cough as Coughing
CURES COUGHS & COLDS

A JEANNE DARC
NOUVEAUTÉS
LIBRAIRIES
ASTRE ET COLA
CARCASSONNE.

Leciferrin
gibt Blut und Kraft
Ovo-Lecithin-Eisen
GALENUS
CHEMISCHE JNDUSTRIE G.m.b.H.
FRANKFURT A.M.

1R. Etre accueilli de vous; et mes vœux sont comblés.
=29 = =49 = 69 =
Ce n'est point à moi à vous répondre.
Tout comme une autre.
Espion
2. Habt. de la Chine.

EL AUTOMOVIL
NUEVA COLECCION DE CANCIONES PARA EL PRESENTE AÑO.
RECOPILADAS POR A. VANEGAS ARROYO. MEXICO.

PRESS
THE SILLY SEASON GOOSEBERRY
RICARDO BROOK

R. HOE & CO.
NEW YORK & LONDON.
No 2 201

Aquarius
Pisces
Aries
Thaurus
Gemini
Cancer
Leo
Virgo
Libra
Scorpius
Sagittarius
Capricornus

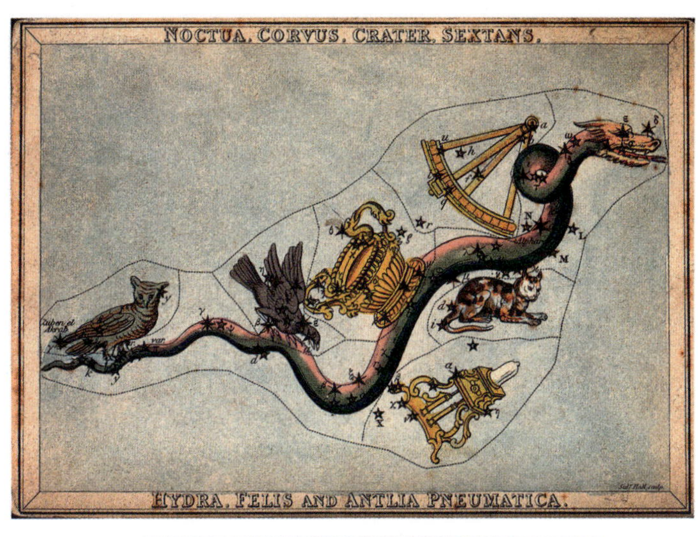
NOCTUA, CORVUS, CRATER, SEXTANS.
HYDRA, FELIS AND ANTLIA PNEUMATICA.

SAGITTARIUS AND CORONA AUSTRALIS.

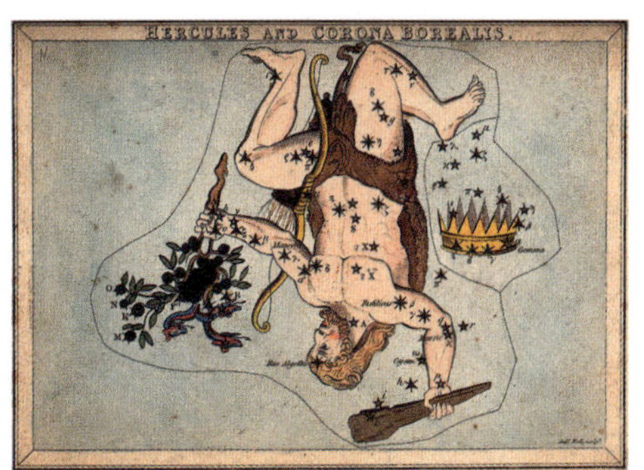
HERCULES AND CORONA BOREALIS.

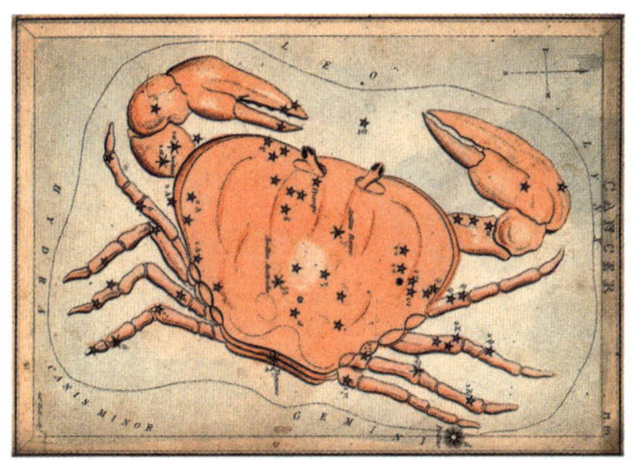

DELPHINUS, SAGITTA, AQUILA,
AND ANTINOUS.

CEPHEUS

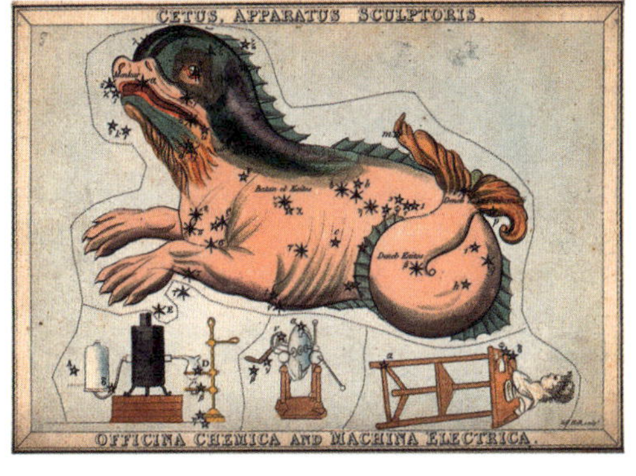
CETUS, APPARATUS SCULPTORIS,
OFFICINA CHEMICA AND MACHINA ELECTRICA.

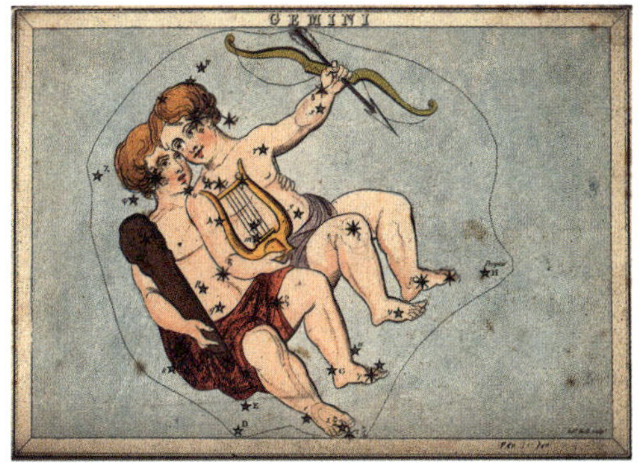
GEMINI

10

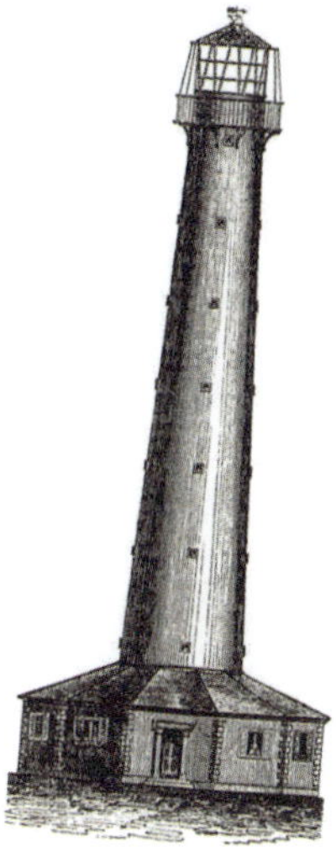
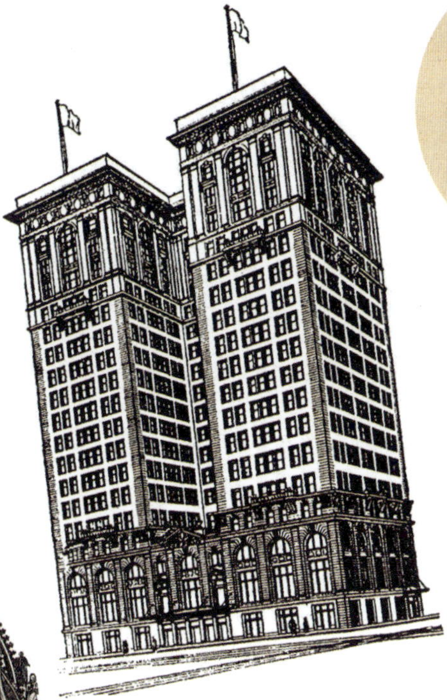
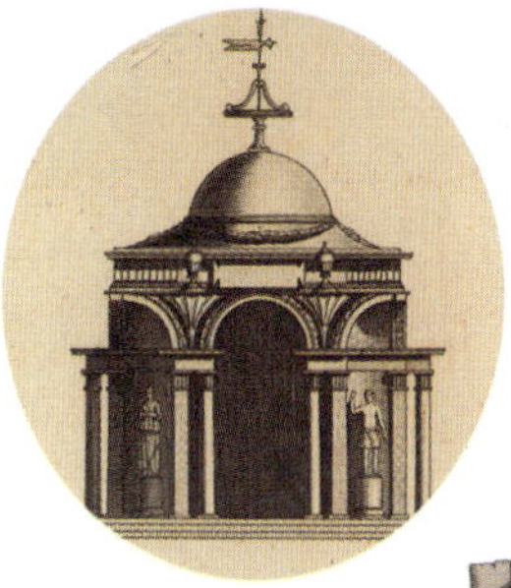
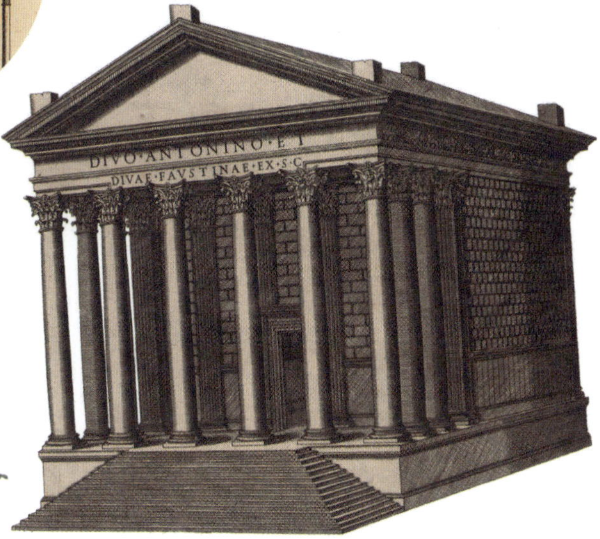
DIVO·ANTONINO·ET
DIVAE·FAVSTINAE·EX·S·C
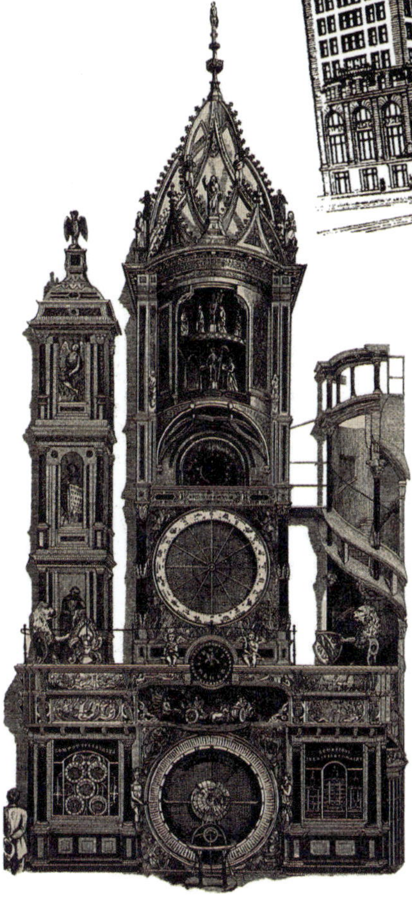
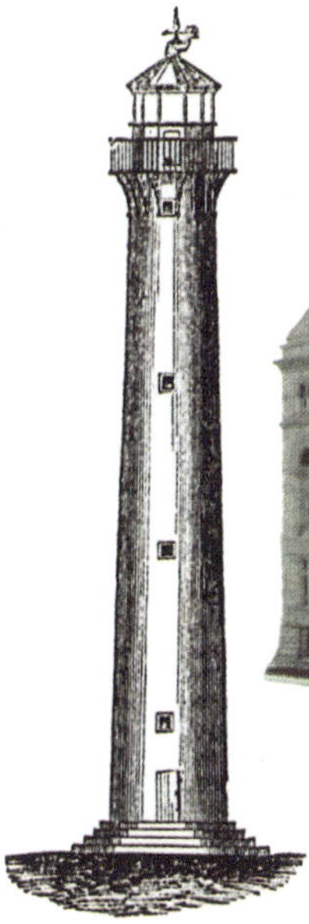
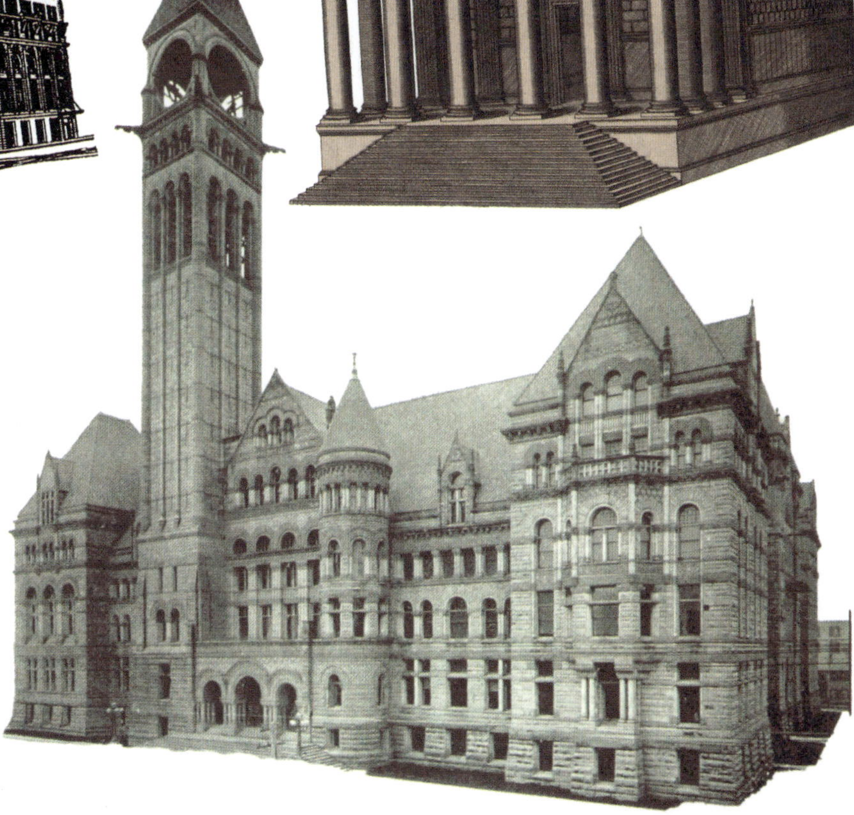

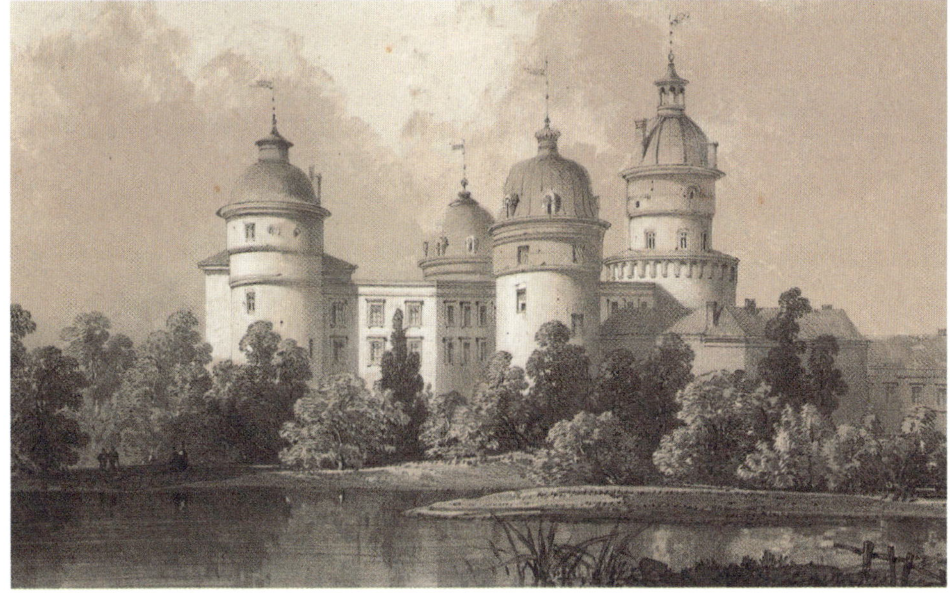

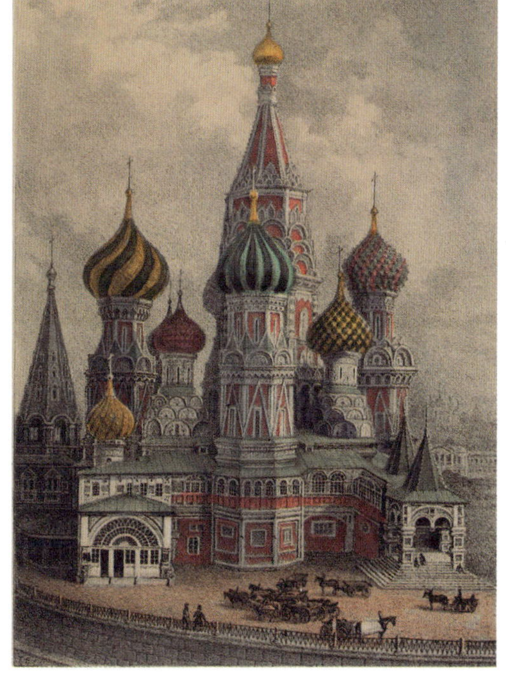

D·BARNASCONI
AMSTERDAM
NOUVEAUTÉS·DE·LA·SAISON
SPÉCIALITÉ·MANTEAUX·ROBES

CIRCULUS MERIDIANUS
HORIZON

JUNG

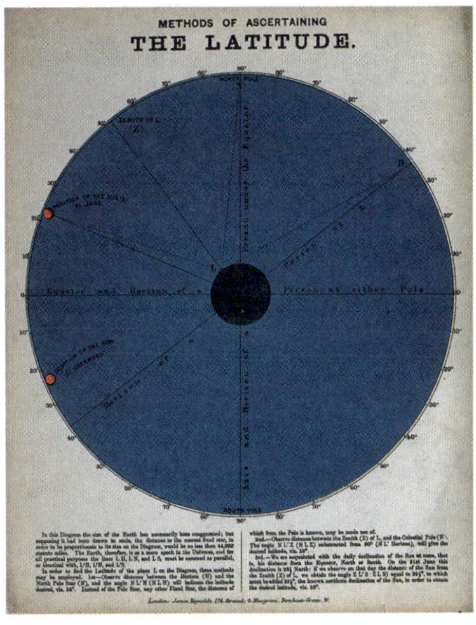
METHODS OF ASCERTAINING
THE LATITUDE.

Circulus Meridianus
HORIZON

Circulus Meridianus
HORIZON

BEATE FRANCISCI SALESI

POMME
KOBOKO

CHOCOLAT
KLAUS

ST-NICHOLAS
CHRISTMAS-NUMBER

Divan Japonais
75 rue des Martyrs
Ed Fournier
directeur

Galerie et Fenêtres
Eglise Notre Dame de Paris
XVe Siècle
Cloître de St Jean des Rois
à Tolède.

O'ROURKE, CATCHER, N. Y

Mr. T. P. COOKE AS NEWTON FOSTER.
No 102
Printed & Sold by M & M SKELT. 11 Swan St Minories London.

ECLIPSE OF THE MOON
The Moon in Opposition
FIG. 1.
SUN
EARTH
MOON
Last contact with Shadow
MOON
First contact with Shadow
Orbit of the Moon
FIG. 2.
MOON
Ecliptic
Moon escapes Eclipse
Moon Partially Eclipsed
Moon Totally Eclipsed

冨嶽三十六景　凱風快晴

北斎改為一筆

ATELIER
F.A. BRIDGMAN